Buttons the Basset

JAMES ROBERT

PAGE PUBLISHING, INC.
Conneaut Lake, PA

First originally published by Page Publishing 2020

ISBN 978-1-64701-727-9 (pbk)
ISBN 978-1-64701-729-3 (hc)
ISBN 978-1-64701-728-6 (digital)

Printed in the United States of America

For Maddie Kay

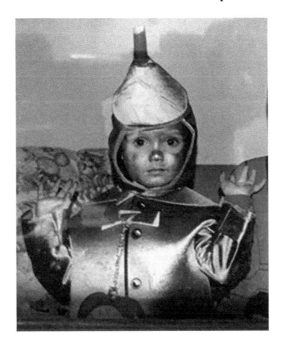

Buttons the Basset awoke early in the morning to search for his bone. After a quick stretch, it was time for him to fetch.

Buttons thought he had left his bone by the door the day before...but something was wrong because the bone was gone.

4

Buttons said to himself, "What will I do? What can I chew?"

As Buttons stared at the floor, he spotted the rubber mat by the door. "What would be wrong with that? Why couldn't I chew the mat?" Buttons chewed and chewed the mat until that was that!

What can I chew?

Buttons kept searching for his bone. He wouldn't leave it alone. He thought to himself, *What will I do? What can I chew?*

Off by the window, Buttons sat, looking at the strangest hat. He thought to himself, *I tried the mat. Now how about the hat?*

Buttons jumped to the floor, and he tore and tore until the hat was no more. *Now what will I do? What can I chew?*

Buttons kept searching for his bone. He wouldn't leave it alone. Off to the closet at the end of the hall, there was simply no time to stall.

Buttons was looking deep through the heap. He found a shoe then began to chew. Thank goodness, it wasn't new!

Now quickly down the stairs, Buttons went. He was hoping to pick up the scent. What should he do? Buttons could find nothing to chew!

21

Suddenly the door flung open, and his dad walked in.

"Buttons, what did you do? What have you chewed! Now go back to your bed. This chewing must end!"

As Buttons lay on his bed, he thought to himself, *This is really quite new. I have nothing to chew.*

Suddenly he felt a strange lump. It was really a big bump. He leaped from his bed and tucked under his head.

There it was, sitting all alone, Buttons had finally found his bone!

Color Buttons.

Help Buttons find his bone.

These are Buttons's favorite bones. What colors are they?

How many bones are in Buttons's bowl?

BUTTON'S SAFETY TIPS FOR HIS FRIENDS:

1. KNOW WHO YOU LIVE WITH AND KNOW YOUR HOME ADDRESS

2. KNOW HOW TO USE THE PHONE.

3. LEARN YOUR PHONE NUMBERS.

4. WHEN THERE IS AN EMERGENCY CALL 911.

5. NEVER GO ANYWHERE WITH PEOPLE YOU DON'T KNOW.

6. NO ONE SHOULD EVER ASK YOU TO KEEP SECRETS. TELL YOUR PARENTS IF THEY DO.

BUTTONS REMINDS US TO:

1. ALWAYS BE KIND TO OTHER PEOPLE.

2. REMEMBER TO SAY PLEASE AND THANK YOU.

3. SHARE WITH OTHERS. THEY MAY NOT HAVE AS MUCH AS YOU.

4. BE THANKFUL FOR WHAT YOU HAVE.

5. YOU ARE A SPECIAL PERSON WITH GIFTS AND TALENTS YOU WILL DISCOVER THROUGHOUT YOUR LIFE.

6. YOUR FAMILY LOVES YOU JUST THE WAY YOU ARE.

7. EACH DAY IS A NEW BEGINNING FILLED WITH CHALLENGES AND NEW ADVENTURES.

This book belongs to _____.

This book was given to me by _____.

I am _____ years old.

My birthday is _____.

Draw a picture of yourself here with Buttons.

About the Author

This is James Robert's second book in a series following the daily adventures of Buttons the Basset Hound. Robert's life's work has been dedicated to Urban Education and helping students achieve their highest potential, as well as building a positive school climate. In his free time, he volunteers and reads at elementary schools. Robert's mission is to promote literacy and encourage students to write their own stories.

CPSIA information can be obtained
at www.ICGtesting.com
Printed in the USA
BVHW020829120421
604255BV00004B/5